Bygones presented by Anglia

CW01658841

A PENNY A B

Norfolk children at work in Victorian days

Sally Livingstone

Illustrated by Martin Knowelden

The Boydell Press · Ipswich

© Sally Livingstone 1978

Published by The Boydell Press Ltd
PO Box 24 Ipswich IP1 1JJ

ISBN 0 85115 104 3

Acknowledgements

I would like to thank Miss Rachel Young for her unfailing help, guidance and gentle criticism, and also Jean and Dick Joice for their unswerving support and encouragement, without which this book might never have been written.

Photoset and printed in Great Britain by
Lowe & Brydone Printers Limited, Thetford, Norfolk

Contents

Foreword

Sally Livingstone worked for Anglia Television for ten years and for nine of those was secretary to me. Anyone who can claim to have done that deserves to be heard – or read! She stopped looking after the administrative side of local programmes three years ago in order to return to College for a teacher training course. A year ago she turned up in my office again and asked if she could borrow some books of old pictures showing children working in the nineteenth century. She told me she wanted them to illustrate a thesis she was writing for her diploma. I asked her if I could see it when it was finished and earlier this year the manuscript arrived on my desk. As soon as I read it I felt that it would be a great pity if it wasn't published. I showed it to Boydell Press and they thought so too. Obviously we were right, for not only is it an interesting and worthwhile piece of work but Sally has qualified as a teacher and is now doing an Honours Degree course.

At least it proves that working for me wasn't that bad, or that she has got even further not working for me!

DICK JOICE

Introduction

Most adults today have memories of childhood which are pleasantly carefree and secure, marred by nothing more disagreeable than perhaps an occasional mild disinclination to go to school or a burning dislike of rice pudding and cabbage. The security, welfare and happiness of children is now one of the major aims of our society. It is recognised that our children are the key to the future, and that every child should be allowed to experience a protected and untroubled period of growth and development and a prolonged, purposeful and even enjoyable education, is no longer questioned.

The use of child labour in the nineteenth century has, therefore, become one of the most distressing and notorious aspects of a period so near to our own that many are still able to recall it and many volumes have been written exposing the exploitation, degradation and cruelty children were subjected to, especially in the rapidly developing industrial cities.

This study looks at Norfolk and attempts to trace the pattern of child labour in the county from the end of the Napoleonic wars in 1815 until the outbreak of the First World War in 1914. As the century progressed the pattern altered and I have tried to show the most significant reasons for that change. It also seeks to illustrate the kinds of occupations in which children were employed, the hours they worked and the wages they earned, not only in the rural areas of Norfolk but also in the city and on the coast.

In looking at the lives of the children of the poor who, for the greater part of the century, could expect to start work sometimes as young as five or six years old, two further questions seemed relevant. Firstly, if and why it was necessary, and secondly, what attitudes and beliefs prevailed in a society which for so many years was prepared to tolerate abuses of small children which today are so totally unacceptable?

Chapter One The Early Years: 1815–1850

"Men of England, wherefore plough
For the lords who lay ye low?
Wherefore weave with toil and care
The rich robes your tyrants wear?"
(Shelley 1819)

Although the nineteenth century was to witness greater changes, technologically, agriculturally, politically and socially, than had ever before occurred within a span of one hundred years, for practically three-quarters of the century the lives of the poor remained almost unchanged.

The last twenty-five years of the eighteenth century saw an increasing preoccupation with the condition of the working man, but there were still many who criticized any early tentative efforts at alleviating his misery, like Joseph Townsend who, in 1783, stated categorically that no "human efforts" could improve the state of the poor and that only hunger could induce "sobriety, diligence and fidelity".[1] Few of the reforming attitudes of the late Victorian era were apparent at the beginning of the nineteenth century, therefore, and it opened as an age of disregard for and exploitation of the poor, coupled often with contempt. It also distinguished itself as an age of extreme piety and one in which it was considered that a man's position in life was pre-ordained and should be endured or enjoyed with grateful acceptance or, in the case of the poor, with meek resignation.

The situation of the labouring poor in Norfolk during the first half of the century can only be described as wretched. Housing both in country and town was inadequate, overcrowded, insanitary and cold; long and physically exhausting hours had to be worked for miserable wages which in no way enabled a man to support his family in even minimal comfort.

In the country enclosures of common land for cultivation deprived the labourer of an important means of easing the demands on the family budget. These areas had previously provided a patch of land on which a pig could be kept or poultry raised. They had also enabled the labourers to snare an occasional rabbit, catch an eel, gather reeds for thatching or wood for kindling, and sometimes clay for their cottages. Their loss meant that men became wholly dependent on earned wages.

Added to this by 1815 increasing numbers of men were returning from the Napoleonic wars swelling the ranks of the working class in a country which had already been affected by an astonishing increase in population. From 1750 to 1801 the population of England and Wales rose from 6½ million to 9 million. In 1811 it was 10 million and by 1821 12 million. This was reflected in the countryside where there were more people between 1800 and 1850 than ever before.

The men who fought and survived the battle of Waterloo returned to a country that was also in the throes of change and whose wealth was increasing rapidly as a result of new methods of manufacture and transport. However, despite these early stirrings of the industrial revolution the villages were still the pivot of life for most Englishmen and the countryside had almost completed its eighteenth century transformation. Agriculture was steadily becoming more efficient and more and more farmers were adopting improved methods of tilling, rotation of crops and stock-breeding. Better methods, however, resulted in a more judicious – and sometimes less regular – use of labour: not a happy moment for the countryside to be undergoing not only a population explosion but a reflux of men returning from the wars.

Fewer jobs and an over-abundance of labour meant that land-owners and farmers could pay lower wages as men were so desperate they were prepared to do any work for any money. The payment of poor relief to supplement wages, which became known as the "Speenhamland system" also benefited the employing farmers whilst, although helping the working man to avoid the immediate threat of starvation, in the long term pauperized and demoralized him. Added to this the high price of food which resulted from the passing of the 1815 Corn Law meant that men were often unable to afford even the basic necessities needed to feed their families.

Life for those who lived in the "closed" villages of Norfolk could be marginally better if the squire was in residence at the hall and did his duty. All the land in a "closed" village was owned by one resident lord of the manor or squire. He was the sole landowner, landlord and employer of the people living in the village and had absolute control over their lives. In many cases housing in these villages was good and there was food, fuel and clothing for all in times of need. For those living in the "open" villages, however, this was usually not the case. In these villages there were many landowners, many employers, no resident squire and therefore no single authority. Cottages were inferior and rents far higher than those on the estates and sanitation and water supplies were frequently inadequate.

The labourer's position in the economic and social life of the village continued to deteriorate until 1834. The Poor Law Amendment Act introduced that year instituted a new system of relief. Boards of Guardians managed groups of parishes linked in Unions and the provision of a workhouse – organized in such a way that it would be a deterrent to rather than a refuge from poverty – was compulsory. The discontent and unrest aroused by these new measures in men already unable to maintain their families manifested itself in incendiary fires, cattle maiming and disturbances in the villages.

The steady decline of the textile industry had deprived many labourers' wives of the piece-work they had previously taken in to alleviate a little of the economic hardship in the cottages of the poor and this was also acutely felt in the city of Norwich.

In Norwich population growth – from 37,256 people in 1811 to 80,368 in 1871 – together with a steady flow of people from the countryside seeking work, put increasing pressure on an already over-crowded city. The worsted weaving industry, at its peak in 1750, which had provided work for so many of the city's poor families, was dying. By 1840 the competition from the Yorkshire machine-made cloths forced Norwich manufacturers to cut production costs and weavers' wages were reduced so drastically that families were in danger of starvation. The boot and shoe industry grew slowly during this period, the brewing industry expanded and a number of large factories were built like The Yarn Company mill at Whitefriars in 1836, but despite this competition for both skilled and unskilled jobs was intense and wages remained pitifully inadequate.

Thus the unavoidable necessity for every member of a family to work, coupled with the absence of any protective legislation or compulsory schooling for children, led to the distressing use and exploitation of child labour on the land and in the cities during the nineteenth century.

It has often been said that the exploitation of children during this period was as much the fault of their parents as of those employing them, but to do so is surely to ignore the pressures and suffering of parents living in indescribable poverty and squalor faced usually with the alternative of watching their children starve or allowing them to work, sometimes almost

as soon as they could walk. The accusation of exploitation and cruelty must, one would think, be unquestionably directed at the politicians, farmers, land and factory owners who continually ignored the plight of the working man and resisted any pleas for wage increases which would have enabled him to support his family in reasonable comfort and shield his children from the hardships they had to endure. For most nineteenth century employers of labour the choice was simple: it was cheaper to employ a child than a man and any job that could conceivably be carried out by a child was therefore given to a child.

In both cases also long familiarity with a situation which caused so much misery and suffering probably dulled and deadened any misgivings or disquieting thoughts. The first stirrings of the social reformers were evident in the early part of the century, however, in the Factory Acts of 1833, 1844 and 1847, but as there were few factories in Norfolk this was of no real significance to the children in the county.

Lord Shaftesbury was the father of all nineteenth century factory legislation as well as being the saviour of the climbing boys used by chimney sweeps. He devoted his life with single-minded religious fervour to the cause of social philanthropy, and yet even he opposed any proposals for compulsory education for children. This reflected an attitude towards the family and parental responsibility current during the Victorian age, for it was thought that any restriction of the right of parents over their children would undermine the stability of the family. Thus, compulsory education, which would have given some protection against the economic exploitation of children, Shaftesbury considered, put at risk the right of a parent to bring up his children as he saw fit. He also thought that it would affect the encouragement of qualities such as personal initiative, responsibility and self-reliance and that a negative attitude of dependency on the State would result. With such prevailing beliefs and attitudes it was therefore not surprising, or particularly noteworthy, that in 1830 Parliament decided to allocate £70,000 towards the building of the Royal stables, and the princely sum of £30,000 to the voluntary organizations which were attempting to educate the children of the masses.[2]

This rigid and uncompromising attitude towards parental rights and responsibility was not reserved just as an expedient in agriculture and industry to resist attempts to prevent the exploitation of children, it was also reflected in the behaviour of the middle-class and wealthy towards their own children. In the homes of the privileged, parental domination was absolute, and children in even the wealthiest families were often subjected to a spartan, "character building" regime which involved relegation to cold and cheerless nurseries and strict codes of behaviour which frequently included a beating for dissident childish behaviour.

To dismantle this entrenched philosophy towards children and the poor which had been partly inherited from the eighteenth century and which had been developed – in a contradictory manner – by the Victorians' zealous pursuit of religion inspired by the Calvinistic beliefs and attitudes towards children of men such as Wesley, would take more than a century. "The sins of the father shall be visited on his children" was the answer for most pious upper-class Victorians to the problem of the starving children of the poor.

Necessity created by poverty and the lack of any statutory protection for a child, were the reasons for the labouring children of the nineteenth century and in Norfolk – as in other parts of the country in rural areas and industrial cities – thousands of children worked long and debilitating hours from an early age for the shilling or two that might mean the difference between survival, starvation or the Workhouse to their families.

Chapter Two The Middle Period: 1850–1875

Despite the Factory Acts no further legislation or changes in the law had been instigated by the 1850s which gave children protection against the exploitation of employers or parents in work situations.

In Norfolk they were still a necessary and indispensable part of the family wage-earning unit as the low wages of both the city and agricultural poor could not hope to meet the cost of even the most basic and essential necessities of life for a family. They were also a vital part of the agricultural work-force and fulfilled innumerable domestic and menial functions in households and city trades and industries at a minimum cost to their employers.

A. *IN THE VILLAGES*

> *"The sheep get up and make their many tracks*
> *And bear a load of snow upon their backs,*
> *And gnaw the frozen turnip to the ground*
> *With sharp quick bite, and then go noising round*
> *The boy that pecks the turnips all the day*
> *And knocks his hand to keep the cold away*
> *And laps his legs in straw to keep them warm*
> *And hides behind the hedges from the storm."*
> (Sheep in Winter: John Clare: 1793–1864)

The position of the agricultural labourer and his family became increasingly wretched. A too plentiful supply of labour, when nearly all were dependent on agriculture, and a growing housing shortage in the villages contributed to their hardships. The demise of the spinning industry which had supplemented so many family incomes, and the continued enclosures of common land weighed heavily on men earning so little that many were destitute. Hunger, unemployment and pauperism separated labourers and their families almost completely from other social classes and the chances of a boy or girl improving the position into which they were born were few. For the girls opportunities were not quite so rare. As a rule they stayed at school longer, sometimes until they were twelve or thirteen, and were not so readily

forced into the hard and brutalizing work on the farms which the boys had to endure from very early childhood.

The kind or work which small boys were engaged in on the farms was usually spasmodic and casual, with little or no thought or attempt to train or encourage them in skills which would equip them for more specialized work as they grew older. The jobs were generally seasonal and of short duration and boys were taken out of school, or not sent at all, in order to fulfil a task occurring at specific times in the farming year. Marion Springall described the sort of work a boy might be engaged in:

> "Unless he joined a gang, his first job was usually scaring crows from newly-sown corn. He went into the fields about dawn . . . and remained there until sundown, shouting at intervals, but often engrossed in his solitary games, or in sleeping away the long hours, until an irate master wakened him with blows and angry words. After that there was twitching and weeding corn, singling turnips, and tending the cows in the lanes, until hay-making and harvest, when he led the horses and shouted, 'Hold ye!' to the men on top of the load, as the cart moved on from 'shock' to 'shock'. He might go gleaning with the family unless there were sheep and pigs to tend in the stubble. In the autumn there was potato picking, dibbling wheat, or crow scaring again. In the winter he went stone picking, or pulling and cleaning roots for cattle. Then at the age of twelve he would get regular work as a team-man's boy . . .".[3]

Log Books for Norfolk schools show that this pattern of work continued until the end of the nineteenth century despite educational, agricultural and industrial legislation designed to protect young children.

At Ranworth-with-Panxworth School the record on 5th October, 1874, shows that: "Several boys [were] absent crow-keeping". On 14th October: "A great number of children absent gathering acorns" and by 21st October: "Only nine children present, all the rest after acorns". Acorns were, of course, used to feed the pigs. On 12th October, 1875, Albert Debbage, Walter Debbage, John Saunders and George Daynes were all absent "crow-keeping", and eight years later, on 2nd March, 1883, is seems the Debbage family was still keeping up the tradition of providing crow-scarers as it was recorded. "Noah Debbage absent from school for a few weeks scaring crows".[4]

At Felthorpe School there appears to have been a strong demand for potato "droppers" and pickers in the early spring and autumn, attendances in the early part of October being affected by "Numbers of children . . . wanting early leave to help their parents dig up potatoes". In April, references are made to the effect that: "Attendances for this week [are] very low. Children absent are engaged in 'dropping potatoes' for their parents".[5] Dropping potatoes was nearly always a family occupation, the parents working across the fields dibbling whilst the children followed behind dropping the potatoes into the holes.

Documentary evidence and personal reminiscences show that the hours spent in the fields by children who were under-fed and poorly clothed were cruelly long and the tasks undertaken tedious and often extremely physically hard. The autumn and winter-work was especially gruelling when the weather was bad, and all this for a pitiful wage but one that was essential to eke out meagre family incomes.

Feeding their families was a constant worry to parents and George Baldry and George Edwards have both recalled their memories of breakfast and dinner in their childhood:

> "Salt sop [for breakfast] was a few pieces of bread crumbled into a basin with small pieces of butter, lard or dripping with hot water poured over . . ."

and for dinner:

> ". . . a fine stew of swedes, with Norfolk dumplings steaming hot . . .".
>
> George Baldry[6]

> "My mother . . . would get up in the morning and make a little fire to boil some water. With this she would soak a little bread and a small piece of butter. . . . For dinner I had, day after day for weeks, nothing but two slices of bread, a small piece of cheese, and an apple or an onion".
>
> George Edwards[7]

No allowances were made for the age of the children they employed by their masters. Rolf, 'The King of the Norfolk Poachers', wrote late in his life:

> "You will hear many an old man say he went to work at seven year old, and did not know a letter in the book . . . they went to work in them days so young that they never practized reading or riting, and so forgot all that they had lerned. Wen they were done with the day they were only too ready to eat there megre tea and get them to bed, haven been on the farm from six in the morning till six at night. There were no limited hours for youngsters then, and men did not favour them, there was the word and the blow – and mostly the blow came first".[8]

George Edwards, who was born in Marsham in 1850, the youngest of seven children, described the life of his family in his autobiography. At his birth his mother, father and six children were living in a two-bedroomed cottage. His father's wage as a bullock worker had been reduced to 7s 0d for a seven-day week, which meant leaving home in the morning before it was light and not returning in the evening until it was dark. Despite the Repeal of the Corn Laws in 1851 the condition of the family did not improve and when the Crimean War broke out in 1854 food rose to famine prices. At this time his father was earning 8s 0d for a seven-day week, but with bread costing 1s 0d for a 4 lb loaf, sugar at 8d a lb, tea 6d an ounce and cheese at 1s 6d a lb it is obvious that any possibility of a father alone being able to maintain his family adequately was remote. Consequently by the time George Edwards was four years old his brothers Joseph and John, aged twelve and ten years, were both working for wages of 1s 6d and 1s 2d a week. His sister was helping his mother with hand-loom weaving piece-word by filling bobbins, two of his step-brothers were apprenticed to the carpentering and joinery trade and the third had gone to sea. The absolute necessity for children of the agricultural poor to work is clearly illustrated in the description of this family in the 1850s.

In 1855 George's father was arrested for taking turnips from the farmer's field in an attempt to feed his family. He was convicted and sentenced to fourteen days hard labour and the family was taken into the workhouse. As a convicted thief no farmer would employ him on his release from prison, but he brought his family out of the workhouse and eventually found employment brick-making. Many men and boys were employed in this local trade when work on the farms was scarce and George Baldry has recalled his memories of the brickyards as a boy of twelve "catching" and barrowing the hot bricks from the kiln for 2s 6d a week:

> "Worked from six in the morning till six at night, barrering and setting on the hale, careful to keep the lines straight, handling each brick made three times. . . . Got on fine with catching the bricks, once I had got the way of it, and did not notice that the hot rough edges had worn away the skin of my fingers till I sees the blood oozing out . . .".[9]

When his father came out of the workhouse George Edwards was six years old and was able to find his first job. He was paid 1s 0d for a seven-day week scaring crows from the fields of a nearby farm. He vividly describes the results of his first misdemeanour:

> "Having to work long hours, I had to be up very early in the morning, soon after sunrise, and remain in the fields until after sunset. One day, being completely worn out, I unfortunately fell asleep. . . . Soon after the farmer arrived on the scene and caught me asleep, and for this crime at six years of age he gave me a severe thrashing and deducted 2d from my wage at the end of the week".[10]

A variety of jobs followed when the need for crow-scaring ended. He looked after the cows to prevent them escaping from the fields; he was involved with the whole family in the harvest; he helped his father in the brickfields and cleaned turnips in the winter. This must have been a particularly arduous job for children and he remembers again the harsh treatment received by the boys at the hands of their masters.

> "Well can I remember the many sore backs I had given me by the old steward, who never missed an opportunity to thrash me if I did not clean enough turnips. . . . The treatment I received was no exception to the rule, all poor boys in those days were treated badly. One farmer I knew used to hang the poor boys up by the heels and thrash them on the slightest provocation . . .".[11]

At 8½ years old George Edwards started his first job as a horseman, leading the fore-horse in the drill, and a liking for and aptitude with horses enabled him to continue with this work until he was expert at ploughing at the very young age of ten. Yet, despite the skill and expertise required for a job of this nature, his wages at 13 years of age were still only 2s 9d a week.

The only time of the year when the labourers and their families were in a comparatively strong position was on the eve of harvest when their availability as a big work force was essential to the farmers. Harvest meant certain employment for the whole family and from June till September the child labour force reached its maximum size. Once harvest began speed and efficiency was essential and the innumerable tasks which needed to be performed were too many for the regular work force on the farms. There was work at this time for men, women and children and each task was urgent. Boys and girls helped to make bands and with binding and stooking and young lads and small boys usually led the wagons when carting. George Edwards described his part in the work at harvest.

> "Women were engaged to tie up the corn and the little boys made bonds with which to tie the corn. . . . When the wheat was carted I led the horse and shouted to the loaders to hold tight when the horse moved."[12]

Arthur Randell and Walter Barrett have also recalled their work as young boys in the Fen harvest fields at the turn of the century, and it would appear that the situation had changed little from that which existed in the 1850s.

> "My parents had harvested on the same farm for many years and as soon as we children were able to do so we had to take our share in . . . making the bands to tie the corn and then, as we got older, to tie and shock alongside our elders . . .".[13]
>
> Arthur Randell

> "I was taken to a field of wheat where a six sailed reaping machine, with four horses attached, was waiting . . . I was to ride the offside front horse, keeping it close to the standing corn . . . I spent three weeks riding the reaping horse, then I was switched over to leading the horse and shouting 'Hold tight'."[14]
>
> Walter Barrett

Entries in the School Log Books also reflect the importance of the harvest and show that even when children – especially the girls – were not directly employed in the fields they often had to take care of younger brothers and sisters at home whilst their mothers went to the hay fields. There were those also who frequently had to leave school early in order to carry refreshment to their parents in the fields.

On 7th July, 1882, at Westacre School the teacher recorded: "Several children who passed Standard I and II last Examination away Haymaking. I have sent notices to their parents but without effect . . .".[15] At Snetterton

National School in August, 1883, the record reads: "School thinly attended. Most of the elder children engaged in the harvest field", and in the week beginning 9th August, 1875: "Attendance very poor owing to the commencement of harvest . . .". Again, in June, 1894: "Haytime having commenced, afternoon school is carried on from 1–3.15 as some children are required to carry food and drink to the Fathers and Brothers in the fields, while others are absent to lead the horses".[16] At Felthorpe School on 14th July, 1879, the same problem was occurring: ". . . Several children are absent this week owing to the hay; and to carry dinner to their parents . . .".[17]

When the harvest was over the children and women would start on the all important task of gleaning. After the work in the fields was finished and the harvest was in farmers would allow the labourers' families to scour the fields collecting any grain left lying in the stubble. This small bonus gave some protection against the winter ahead, for wheat gleanings provided flour for bread-making and chickens and pigs could be fed with the barley gathered. The importance of this activity is again reflected in School Log Books. As late as 8th September, 1890, the teacher of Westacre School wrote: "Tried to re-open School but gleaning not being nearly finished was unable to do so, and owing to wet weather the Harvest is unfinished".[18] At Snetterton National School on Friday, 7th August, 1874: "School closed, gleaning having commenced", and in 1876 on 9th August: "School closed for 4 weeks holidays. Gleaning commenced".[19]

It is clear from these records that school teachers were unable to combat the economic necessity of the harvest and gleaning to poor families and many adjusted their time-tables accordingly during the crucial months between June and September.

Although most of the menial casual and seasonal tasks on farms were usually considered to be boys' work there is much evidence to show that young girls also were often employed in crow-scaring, turnip picking and cleaning, stone picking, gathering acorns and dropping and picking potatoes. It was thought, however, that the field labouring girl would inevitable be coarsened by her work, which necessarily took place alongside men and boys, and that this would eventually make her unfit both for domestic service and for marriage. In 1867, T. H. Harrison, a Norfolk headmaster, giving evidence before the Agricultural Employment Commissioners, said: "I could not recommend a girl for domestic service who had been habituated to field work".[20]

Domestic service was considered to be the most respectable and suitable employment for poor girls and W. J. Reader concluded that:

> "The best thing a cottager's daughter could hope for was to go into service in a good family, and when she was between ten and fifteen years old her parents would try to place her".[21]

Occasionally boys, too, were employed on the larger farms or estates as servants, their duties usually involving work in the garden, carrying coal, cleaning knives and boots and other miscellaneous duties. But for young girls going into service was the brightest prospect they could hope for although this often entailed leaving their homes to work in houses long distances from their families, with few opportunities to visit or see their parents and brothers and sisters again. The Westacre School Log Book reveals one such case when, on 30th September, 1890, "Lily Pitcher left for service at Yarmouth . . .".[22]

Although these enforced separations from their families must have afforded considerable distress and anxiety to young girls and the work they were required to do was often hard and tiring, if the position found was with a good and considerate family they must surely have benefited from their much improved living conditions. Presents of a dress or winter coat were often given by employers to their servant girls at Christmas, as well as material for underwear and uniforms of caps, aprons and dresses if these were required to be worn. Food was always provided and was probably inevitably more plentiful, varied and nutritious than that which they would have enjoyed at home, and many young servant girls often sent up to half of their very small wage back to their families in an effort to alleviate a little of their suffering.

Families with seven to ten children were the norm and with too little room in their cottages – children sometimes sleeping four or five to a bed – and too many mouths to feed it is easy to understand why the advantages of finding a "good place" for a daughter "in service" were so apparent to the poor. Unless,

therefore, a girl was needed to look after younger brothers and sisters at home, efforts were usually made to secure such a position as soon as a girl was considered old enough.

Apart from actual paid employment the young daughters of poor labouring families were also needed to do many of the household tasks in order to release their mothers so that they might earn money to supplement the family income either on the farms of by doing piece-work at home, perhaps for the weaving industry. This might mean caring for the younger children., carrying water, washing, or preparing food for the family. Work of this nature must have been very hard and arduous for girls of ten and eleven and would in no way be expected of children of that age today. Sometimes they might also help the mother with her paid work, as George Edwards' sister did in filling the bobbins which his mother used.

Perhaps the most notorious and distressing aspect of child labour in the 1850s was the agricultural "gang", a system of labour which originated and largely operated in East Anglia and the Midlands. The gangs, which were known as "jobbing", "common" or "travelling" gangs were made up mainly of women and children and were worked under a gang-master, who hired the work force out on contract to any farmer requiring help. The size of the gangs usually ranged between twenty and forty members and children as young as five and six could be found in their numbers. The work undertaken was varied and seasonal and included tasks like picking "twitch", weeding, hoeing, spreading manure, setting and sorting potatoes, singling turnips and stone picking. The gangs sometimes had to travel long distances on foot to reach their place of work and the hardship and privation endured by very small children must have been severe. They often worked as many as fourteen hours a day and walked perhaps five, six or more miles before they even started their work and the same distance back again at night. The gang-masters, reputedly not the most humanitarian of men, were usually paid on a piece-work basis and with a contract to meet worked the gangs hard with no respite. The members of a gang were hired by the day and a full day's work had to be completed or pay was withheld. A child could earn 1½d a day at the age of six, rising to 7d or 8d earned by the women.

A Parliamentary Report on the Employment of Women and Children in Agriculture 1843 brought to light the existence of the Castleacre "gangs". Castleacre was an "open" village where many of the poorer families congregated, living in ghetto-like conditions, and it was to these "open" villages that the farmers looked to supplement their work forces when "closed" villages could not provide sufficient labourers to meet their needs. The gang system was at its height between 1840 and 1870, but by 1866 was causing sufficient concern to Victorian reformers for a Commission of Inquiry to be held. In 1867 The Children's Employment Commission produced evidence which showed that approximately 1,000 children between the ages of six and thirteen were employed in gangs in Norfolk.[23]

The father of an eleven year old child who had been working in a gang for two years gave this evidence to the Commission.

"I'm forced to let my daughter go, else I'm very much against it. . . . She has complained of pain in her side very often; they drive them along – force them along – they make them work hard. Gathering stones has hurt my girl's back at times. Pulling turnips is the hardest work; they get such a hold of the ground with their roots; when the land's strong it's as much as we can do to get 'em out, pull as hard as we can pull. It blisters their hands so that they can hardly touch anything. . . . My girl went 5 miles yesterday to her work, turniping; she set off between seven and eight, she walked; had a piece of bread before she went; she did not stop work in the middle of the day; ate nothing till she left off; she came home between 3 and 4 o'clock. Their walks are worse than their work; she is sometimes so tired, she can't eat no victuals when she comes home".[24]

The Gangs Act which was passed in 1867 made some attempt to protect very little children from the exploitation, hardship and moral dangers endemic in the system by prohibiting the employment of any child under eight years of age. It also required that gang-masters should be licensed by a local magistrate; that public gangs of mixed sex were illegal and that a gang-mistress should be present where gangs were composed of women and girls. Nevertheless evasions of the law continued to occur after 1867 and private gangs, not covered by the Act, were often used by farmers.

Agriculture and domestic service provided work for the largest proportion of children in Norfolk up to the end of the century – the 1871 Census showing that over 5,000 boys between the ages of five and fourteen were employed as farm labourers, farm servants or shepherds. But the Census also revealed that a tiny proportion were employed in the traditional rural crafts. In the same age range there were 67 blacksmiths, 12 saddlers, 64 carpenters and joiners, and 9 wheelwrights.[25]

For the poor children who lived in the fishing villages and ports which are scattered picturesquely down Norfolk's coastline from Hunstanton to Great Yarmouth, life was as hard and uncertain as for those living in the city and country. Many of them worked on the land and in service, but there were alternative occupations connected with the sea and fishing which added an even greater degree of uncertainty to their lives. There were few families living on the coast who had not suffered the loss of a boy or man through drowning.

During the nineteenth century Norfolk men were involved in the hazardous business of whale fishing off Greenland and Davis Strait, the Yarmouth herring industry still flourished and boats from Sheringham and Cromer engaged in deep-sea fishing, crabbing and herring and mackerel fishing. Lobsters, mussels, whelks and cockles were also harvested from the sea. If the fishing was bad then the people on the coast suffered, pantries emptied and belts had to be tightened.

Virtually the entire community of a coastal village would usually be involved in one way or another with the fishing industry. There were nets, whelk and lobster pots to be made, rope to be woven, boats to be built and repaired and numerous other crafts and tasks inseparably interwoven with the business of fishing.

For the boys it was almost inevitable that they would follow their fathers and brothers, often going to sea at a very young age. Sally Festing interviewed many old fishermen for her book on the Norfolk fishing industry and people, most of whom remembered how their fathers and grandfathers started life at sea.

Seventy-five year old Jo Pegg related how his father went to sea at seven as a cabin boy and *his* father was a whale catcher. He also described the stone picking gangs at Sheringham in the 1880s. At that time ". . . there would be 40 or 50 children picking the stones and carrying them to boats waiting on the sands for the tide . . .".[26] "Loady" Cox, also 75, remembered leaving school at twelve and helping his father in the whelk sheds. He first went to sea when he was "eight or nine", but asserted that he "Didn' do it for a liven" until he was "fourteen or fifteen".[27] Philip Green, now in his mid-sixties described how his ". . . father ran away to sea when he was eleven or twelve because he thought he'd get more grub there than he did at home".[28] He recalled too how his father as a boy used to collect buckets of horse manure from the lanes to be used when the boats were refitted or patched in the spring. Chalk would also be collected from the pit or alongside the road and this would be ground up and mixed with tar and, together with the horse muck, used to patch and fill cracks in the boats.

Although most of the boys would inevitably have been concerned with the livelihood obtained by their families from fishing and the sea some, too, would certainly have worked on the coastal farms and have encountered and endured the same hardships as those working further inland. Seventy-eight year old "Laddy" Lane described his experiences on the farm as late as the beginning of this century.

> "I used to work weekends when I was eleven . . . I left school when I was twelve or thirteen and worked for 4s 6d a week, that was seven days, milking cows . . . Old Sachel came round with a stick sometimes. I remember once we were loading oats, handing down huge bags and I was too little to take them. The oats fell out and he was after me so I just left".[29]

The evidence suggests that young girls did not play a part in the business of the boats and fishing itself, although it is probable that they helped their mothers with their tasks when mending and drying the nets and perhaps in gathering winkles, cockles and mussels from the shore. As soon as they were old enough, however, domestic service was again the aim of most parents for their girls and when a place was found they were sent away to work in the kitchens or houses of the middle-class and wealthy. The very large houses and estates needed enormous staffs to run them and at a time when even a well-to-do tradesman could afford one or two servants, it was usually not too difficult to find a place, although it might mean travelling a long way from the small village of their birth.

An example of the distances some girls travelled to their places in service is found in Philip Green's reminiscences about his mother, who was born in Stiffkey.

> ". . . Look at my mother, she was buggered off down to the Isle of Wight with a ticket tied onto her coat when she was eleven. Sent down there as a kitchen maid. The train coming into Wells was about the most exciting thing she'd ever seen before that. The donkey and cart took her from here to Wells station because they just couldn't keep them at home . . .".[30]

B. *IN THE CITY*

> *Little Nellie Cassidy has got a place in town,*
> *She wears a fine white apron,*
> *She wears a new black gown,*
> *An' the quarest little cap at all with straymers hanging down.*
> *Little Nellie Cassidy earns fourteen pounds and more,*
> *Waiting on the quality,*
> *And answering the door –*
> *But her heart is somewhere far away upon the Wexford shore.*
> (Winifred M. Letts)

The economic and living conditions of the poor in the city of Norwich in the 1850s were no better than those of their fellows who lived in the country. The textile industry, an important source of work for poor families, had waned over the previous twenty years and a steady flow of people from the countryside who were physically fitter, used to low wages and consequently more suited to unskilled labour than the textile workers, aggravated the problem of housing and increased the competiton for jobs.

Although not as bad as in the big industrial cities, living conditions were appalling. The houses of the poor were mostly concentrated together north of the river on parishes like St Martin-at-Oak. They were to be found mainly living in houses in the Yards, which were owned by private developers and as a rule were narrow, dark and over-crowded. Private ownership meant that the City had no control over the Yards and removal of rubbish was infrequent and it was left to accumulate in piles until it was sold by the developers to farmers as "town muck". There were also the artisan cottages situated at places like New Lakenham, a notorious area, where there were hundreds of houses with no drainage or sanitation.

Life for working-class families was again wretched and often violent and children were sent out to work or worked at home, as they did in the country,

in order that families might survive at mere subsistence level. There are no government reports specifically related to the children who worked in the city of Norwich, but evidence obtained from the Norwich Census of 1851 gives some indication of the range and variety of work that children were usually engaged in. It also reflects some of the trades which the city was most concerned with during this period.

From very early times Norwich was a cattle market and the boot and shoe industry grew out of the leather working trade. There were hundreds of shoe-makers making shoes to measure and the work was usually controlled by a garret master who took orders, bought the leather, cut the shoes out, and then put the work "out" to be finished by several processes. This was done by families by hand in their homes, or in small workshops nearby, and the Norwich Census shows that many children were engaged in the trade. Samuel Melvin, 10 years old, William Walls, 13, and William Roper, 13, lived in Cowgate Street, St Martin-at-Palace, and all three are described as shoe-makers. In Worlds End Lane William Earley, 12 years old, was a shoe-maker and Mack Billan, also 12, a boot closer. The children who lived in the Yards of St Martin-at-Oak were also engaged in the trade. John Cooper lived in White Lion Yard and at 11 years old was described as a shoe-maker, as was 11 year old Robert John Daniel, who lived in Bath House Yard.[31]

It is not clear whether children actually received a wage for this work as often a whole family would help with a father's job in order to complete it more speedily, although the man alone would be paid. This might also have applied to the many girls described as silk, cotton and yarn fillers; for example, Hannah Green, 10 years old, living in Plummers Yard, a silk filler, Elizabeth Rose, Oak Street, 9 years old, a yarn filler, Jane Cozens, the eldest child of six, 12 years old, a cotton filler living in Flower Pot Yard, and Sophia Hornsby, living in Queen Caroline Yard, 12 years old, a bobbin filler.[32] All of these girls could well have been assisting their parents with their work without receiving any pay themselves.

The Census also shows that the city must have been filled with a great many boys and girls running errands. There is scarcely a yard or a street which does not have a boy or girl between the ages of 10 and 13 whose occupation is given as an errand boy or girl. There were, too, a number of children living in the Yards who are described as factory workers and they were probably employed in industries like The Yarn Mill at Whitefriars, machine spinning.[33]

There seems to have been a very great variety of jobs considered suitable for children, some of the occupations sounding extremely adult, like Fred. Thos. Buttle of Palace Plain who, at 13 years old, was a waterman, and William Simonds of Worlds End Lane, a fishmonger at 11. There were also children employed as rag sorters, pill box makers, reel polishers, wool combers and labourers. In Queen Caroline Yard there is an example of a family with eleven children which was involved in the textile industry. All of its members who were old enough were engaged in weaving, the father being described as a weaver and four children between the ages of 10 and 14 as weaver's assistants.[34]

There are numerous recordings in the Census of little girls like Lydia Walker, aged 10, of Worlds End Lane, whose occupation was listed as "a nurse".[35] This description in no way reflects the profession of the nurses of today. These girls were nursemaids, which sometimes simply meant that they child-minded for a neighbour or for their own family. This was probably so in Lydia Walker's case as she was still living at home. Very often though young girls did become nursemaids in the houses of middle-class and wealthy people, as opposed to going into general domestic service, and at the time of the 1851 Census Florence Nightingale was to note that ". . . nearly one-half of all the nurses, in domestic service, [were] between 5 and 20 years of age".[36] This could only mean that in numerous cases very small children were put in positions of responsibility caring for other – more fortunate – small children.

There is evidence also in the Census to suggest that many young girls were required to work within the home, perhaps in order to allow mothers to pursue occupations which would supplement the family income. Both Mary Wright, 13, and Ann Wright, 10, of Worlds End Lane, are listed as being servants at home.[37]

One of the most cruel and unnecessary ways in which small boys were exploited during this period was in their use as "climbing boys" for chimney sweeps. Charles Kingsley wrote about them in "The Water Babies" in 1863 and Lord Shaftesbury fought so successfully on their behalf in the second half of the century that in 1875 an Act of Parliament was passed prohibiting their employment for this purpose. This was a hundred years after Jonas Hanway (1773) made public the terrible ordeals and accidents children were exposed to when climbing chimneys. There were cases of boys being badly beaten in order to "persuade" them to climb; of fires being lit in the grates beneath them for the same purpose; and of knees and elbows being treated with brine to toughen them for climbing. Many of these children died through suffocation or being overcome by fumes in chimney flues. A further indictment of the inhumanity of this practice was in the fact that even in 1773 it would have been possible to use machines for cleaning chimneys.

Norfolk must have had its quota of climbing boys in the nineteenth century and Jamesina Waller has recalled her memory of one such boy:

> "I distinctly recall the half terror of the poor sooty boy standing on a dust sheet on the floor and Mother holding my hand while she led me up to him and obliged me to put a thick piece of Bread and Butter into his hand, then my astonishment at his thanking us and devouring it".[38]

As in the country, domestic service in the households of the rich and middle-class was an important and respectable source of work for the children of the poor. Its respectability and suitability is illustrated by the records kept by the Committees of the Girls' and Boys' Homes attached to the Norwich Workhouse. The division of the pauper children and adults into separate homes came about as a result of the 1834 Poor Law Amendment Act, and was an attempt to eradicate with a more positive approach what were considered to be the self-perpetuating habits of pauperism and the workhouse. In order to achieve this the children were to be given some basic instruction in reading and writing and the principles of the Christian religion, and further instruction which would "train them to habits of usefulness, industry and virtue".[39] To help facilitate this aim provision was made for the appointment of a school-master and a school-mistress in each union workhouse. Sadly "habits of usefulness and industry" were usually only encouraged by the girls being required to help with domestic and household duties and the boys with jobs in the workhouse gardens.

Nevertheless, it is apparent from the Committee Notes of the Norwich Homes that attempts were made to place the children in positions which would assure a reasonable future, and that some "after-care" was practised in the form of inquiries into the fulfilment of conditions of employment if there were any – for example, the teaching of a trade or the proper payment of wages. Another early attempt at "after-care" was the Working Boys' Home, opened in 1846 by the Board of Guardians of Norwich Union. This Home provided subsidised accommodation for former workhouse boys who were then employed, but whose earnings were not sufficiently adequate to allow them to maintain themselves properly.

Extracts from the Committee Book of the Boys' Home attached to the Norwich Workhouse in 1856 illustrate the sort of positions the boys were placed in. On 2nd May it was ordered:

> "That Albert Keetch from the School be admitted into the Home and go to service with Mr. G. W. Minns at 2/- a week. That Thomas Howes be also admitted into the Home and go to service with Mrs. Cole, Newmarket Road, in place of George Flaxman at 1/- a week and Board. That John Sharp who has left Mr. Robinson go to service with Mr. Long, Mount Pleasant, at 1/- a week, his Dinner and outside clothing (except shoes)".[40]

Boys placed as "indoor servants" usually started at 1/- a week and their keep, and all boys when leaving the Home were, as a rule, given a cloth or corduroy suit.

A later entry in the same year gives an example of the attempts at "after-care":

> "The Master reported that Mr. Challis had declined to increase William Watling's wages. Ordered that Mr. Lingwood again sees Mr. Challis and inform him that unless he will teach the Boy his Trade or increase his wages he is to leave at the end of a month".[41]

This seems to have been of no avail, however, as on 31st August this entry appeared:

> "The Master reported that Mr. Challis had declined to teach William Watling the Trade of a Boot-maker or increase his wages and that Watling desired to leave the Home and endeavour to maintain himself".[42]

Wage increases for the boys continued to concern the Committee as this minute for 2nd January, 1857, shows. It was ordered:

"That the Master of the Home be empowered to [speak] to the Masters of such boys whom he considers are entitled to an increase of wages".[43]

There were obviously considerable problems associated with placing some of the boys, not the least being their behaviour. On 1st May, 1857, it was noted that:

". . . Joseph Craig had gone into the employment of Mr. Ashton, Whipmaker, at 2s 6d a week . . .".[44]

But by 29th May Joseph Craig had been ". . . discharged for dishonesty and sent by order of the Governor to the Workhouse . . .".[45]

On 30th September, 1859, an entry read:

"The Master reported William Wenn for insolent conduct and that he wished to go to Sea. Ordered that the Master go to Yarmouth and endeavour to obtain a Berth for William Wenn".[46]

Unfortunately the herring boats of Yarmouth did not provide a solution as on 28th October:

"The Master reported that he had been unable to obtain a berth at sea for William Wenn and recommended under present circumstances his staying in Mr. Pratt's service . . .".[47]

A wider range of potential employment seems to have been open to boys compared with the girls, as the Committee notes show that although many went as servants in the large houes, there were others who were bound to apprenticeships, or placed with masters who would hopefully teach them a trade.

The apprenticeships found for pauper boys were more genuine after the 1834 Poor Law was passed. Before that date boys were often bound to masters for long terms when there was no intention of a trade being taught, but simply to provide cheap labour. The revised Poor Law attempted to eradicate the dangers of exploitation inherent in the apprenticeship system.

Boys were usually apprenticed at about fourteen years of age and examples can be found in the Minute Book of the Norwich Boys' Home.

On 25th December, 1855, it was ordered:

"That Alfred L'Estrange, who is about to be apprenticed to R. W. Bacon, printer, be allowed to remain at the Home for one year."[48]

On 29th February, 1856:

"That Owen Philips now in service with Mr. Munn to go on liking to a plumber and glazier and, if approved, be apprenticed for six years, premium £3 (paid by the churchwardens of his home parish), wages 3/- a week for the first year, plus 1/- a week each year".[49]

There are many other examples, like Vincent Riches, apprenticed to a wine cooper on 28th April, 1856, and also entries betraying philanthropic attitudes in the Home. The record on 29th May, 1857, reveals that 3d a week pocket money had been granted to a boy who was apprenticed to a plumber and already earning 2s 6d a week.[50]

A list of boys from the school who had obtained employment was recorded on 23rd February, 1849, and this also illustrates the diversity of occupations open to them. There were three boys "at sea"; three were "shoe-making"; two were "in haberdashery" – perhaps as shop assistants or errand boys; one was "with a carpenter"; two were "in public houses" – one of whom was "Boots" at The Boar's Head; one was "with a bricklayer" and another "with a dyer at Aylsham".[51]

Domestic service, however, was predominant when placing girls. A typical example of girls being found positions in service is found in the Committee Notes of the Girls' Home on 28th April, 1857.

> "Ordered that Margaret Fox go to service with Mrs. Balls, Newmarket Road, Emily Cadge with Mrs. Smith, Oxford Street, Unthank Road and Florence Allen with Mrs. Clifford, Earlham Terrace and that each girl have the usual allowance of 12s 6d and a pair of shoes".[52]

Entries of this nature are common, and it would appear that "the usual allowance of 12s 6d" was to enable a girl to outfit herself in clothes suitable for the position she was about to take up.

More rare and unusual is the entry for 25th September, 1860, which reads:

> "Ordered upon the recommendation of the Medical Officer that Victoria Howell leave the Home to go to live with Mrs. Mackley, Tailoress who will teach her her business for 12 months and the Relief Committee be recommended to allow her 3/- a week".[53]

It is clear from the Committee Notes that, as with the boys, simply placing the girls in suitable positions did not always mean that their responsibility could end. There were sometimes difficulties. On 27th December, 1859, it was ordered:

> "That Elizabeth Freeman having left her situation for dishonesty be sent to the Workhouse".[54]

It would seem, however, that Elizabeth was given a conditional reprieve as on 31st January, 1860, the record showed that:

> "The Matron reported that Elizabeth Freeman who was at the last meeting ordered to be sent to the Workhouse had by leave of the House Visitor since been sent to service with Mrs. Kidd of Cossey to whom the circumstances of her dishonest practices were made known, which the Committee approved".[55]

The Committee's patience must have been sorely tried on this day as a further entry reads:

> "Also that Matilda Cullum had left Mrs. Roes' service for impertinent behaviour. Ordered that Matilda Cullum remain at the Home for the present".[56]

Impertinent and insolent behaviour were obviously considered to be grave offences, but in an age of extreme religious piety when a man's position in life was constantly being reinforced, even in hymns:

> *The rich man in his castle,*
> *The poor man at his gate,*
> *God made them high and lowly*
> *And ordered their estate.*

it could be wondered what exactly constituted impertinent and insolent behaviour in the eyes of the people employing these children. One wonders, too, precisely what was involved in the "dishonest practices" of Joseph Craig and Elizabeth Freeman. Children in the 1850s were still being sentenced to terms of imprisonment with hard labour usually for crimes of petty theft involving food – hunger, no doubt, being the criminal motive. As there is no statement to the effect that these workhouse children were required to appear before the magistrates, it gives one cause to suspect that the dishonesty was perhaps in the telling of a lie – verbal dishonesty – rather than that these children were imbued with criminal tendencies. Maybe, for instance, Elizabeth Freeman had insisted that she had cleaned and blacked the fire grate when her mistress knew or maintained otherwise. There is certainly no way of telling from the limited information to be gleaned from the Committee Notes.

Life for the children of the poor living in the cities could, therefore, be as hard, cheerless and devoid of childish comforts and pleasures as for those living in the country. That they would work from an early age was inevitable at a time when schooling was not compulsory and the fear of hunger and perhaps starvation ever present in the hovels of the poor. Jobs were perhaps more varied, but the wages were as pitiful and the hours worked as long and exhausting as those of their peers in the country. For the most part also the tasks they had to pursue involved no training or real skill and offered little prospect of improving their situation in life.

Chapter Three The Close of the Century: 1875–1914

". . . the poor man's lot seems to have been so long remembered as to be entirely forgotten."

(From "A Poor Man" 1829–30: John Clare)

There were far fewer children employed on the land and in the cities at the end of the century, although the economic and social plight of the poor had improved only slightly. Some of the reasons for that poverty, however, were different from those that had prevailed earlier.

In 1875 twenty years of successful and intensive farming came to an end and a long and difficult period of agricultural depression followed which increased the hardships of the poor. The area of cultivated land was reduced and farmers economised in order to save labour. Those who were employed worked long, hard hours for farmers who strove to extract every ounce of effort from greatly reduced labour forces. Increasing numbers of young men and women were leaving the villages and migrating to the towns, or emigrating to the new colonies like Canada, and those left behind were unable to resist wage reductions. At the same time the pattern of farming was changing radically as more and more sophisticated machinery began to usurp man-power on the farms.

As the population of the villages began to fall and to age due to the departure of the young men and women driven to the towns in an endeavour to escape from poverty, so the pressures increased on jobs and housing in the cities. In the city of Norwich the situation eased slightly as the century progressed. The steady growth of firms like the Colman Mills and the engineering, brewing and boot and shoe-making industries, had created more jobs in newly built or expanding factories and works. But housing and sanitation were still poor and infant mortality, due mainly to poverty and ignorance, was very high, so much so that in 1873 the first Medical Officer for Health for Norwich stated in his first report that the infant death rate was higher than for any comparable city in the country.

Poverty and need, chief causes of the exploitation of children in work situations, were therefore still miserably apparent, but by the end of the century a flood of reforming legislation, together with the birth of compulsory education, had virtually eliminated the other outstanding cause – the lack of any statutory protection for children.

One of the greatest strengths of mid-Victorian England was perhaps its ability to tolerate and even encourage its own critics, and, as well as the political reformers, men like Shelley, Matthew Arnold, Thomas Carlyle and

Charles Dickens did much to awaken the public conscience to the social and economic evils of the day. Inventiveness, energy, industry and enthusiasm were also characteristics of the era and no generation tackled the social problems of public health, working-class housing, factory conditions and education more vigorously within the methods and knowledge at their disposal than did the mid-Victorians. Reform and legislation, imperfect though it may have been, came thick and fast once the minds of the politicians and upper and middle-classes had been firmly set on the course of remedy and improvement.

The birth and growth of a system of free state education made the biggest impact on the lives of children. The 1867 Reform Act which widened the franchise gave the first real impetus to the beginning of compulsory education for all. It was followed three years later by Forster's Education Act, which was designed to provide elementary education for all poor children by authorising the establishment of rate-aided Board Schools in areas where they were needed. A small fee still had to be paid by parents at this time.

> "I remember starting school at four years old, with my two elder brothers, with our dinner packed in a basket, and sixpence for our education. That was threepence for the eldest, twopence for the second and one penny for myself. My slate and pencil cost 3d . . .".[57]
>
> Burgh St Peter 1884

The School Boards were empowered to impose compulsory school attendance, but as late as 1895 almost twice the number of children attending Board Schools were still receiving their education from voluntary schools of one kind or another. Further steps were taken in 1876 when an Act was introduced requiring the compulsory attendance of all children between the ages of 5 and 10, and between 10 and 13 for those without a certificate showing a certain standard of attainment. This Act also enabled School Boards to establish Attendance Committees to compel parents to send their children to school, but as the power of enforcement was in the hands of local committees who sometimes had a vested interest in children as the cheapest part of their labour force, action depended very much on local conditions.

The 1880 Act which followed laid down that all children between the ages of 5 and 13 should be compelled by law to attend school. This was strengthened by the 1891 Elementary Education Act which made possible free education for all (although it was not until 1918 that school fees were abolished entirely), and the raising of the minimum school leaving age to 11 in 1893 and then to 12 in 1899. This gradual closing of the loop-holes which enabled children to leave school at an early age meant that by 1893–4 approximately three-quarters of 12–13 year old children were still at school.

In addition to the continuing factory legislation and the Agricultural Gangs Act of 1867 already mentioned, the Agricultural Children Act of 1873 also sought to prohibit the employment of children below the age of 8 in agriculture and to ensure minimum school attendance for those aged 8–12, but this was largely ineffective.

Throughout the last quarter of the century, therefore, the child labour force in Norfolk was slowly but steadily eroded by the increasing statutory protection given to children by the State, and also by the technological advances which were enabling farmers to use more machinery and less labour on the land. The introduction of the mechanical reaper and binder gradually transformed the harvest situation which had previously involved men reaping, women gathering the corn and forming the "shocks" and small children making the bands for fastening. This benefited the regular farm labourer as he was able to earn more money in the form of overtime at harvest, but it meant that the employment of the village families, together with other casual labour, individual or in gangs, gradually became less necessary. However, despite the introduction of new farming methods and the advances made in compulsory education there is still evidence to suggest that children continued to help with the harvest right up until the beginning of the First World War. The records kept in the School Log Books already mentioned show that certainly in the 1890s many of the older boys were still being kept away from school to help in the hayfields, children continued to be absent carrying dinner and tea to their fathers and brothers, and school time-tables were being adjusted to accommodate the period of gleaning which continued to be vital to the agricultural workers' livelihood.

By the 1870s an official inquiry put the agricultural labourer's average national wage at 14s 8d a week, with regional variations, and this remained fairly static – 14s 0d or 15s 0d still being general in 1914. The Account Book kept at Testerton Hall Farm in Norfolk for 1899–1900 shows an average labourer's wage of around 13s 6d with a regular work force of approximately twenty-five men. Usually about four boys were also employed on the farm and the record reveals the kind of work they were doing. For example, "Boy" Betts earned 6s 0d doing "yard jobs" during the week ending 1st December, 1899, and "Boy" Wilkin received 3s 6d for scaring crows for the week ending 5th January, 1900. During the week ending 6th July, 1900, "Boy" Longman helped in the garden and "led horse" in the harvest field and received 4s 9d.[58] There are many other examples and it is clear that these boys were in full-time employment as their names appear in the weekly record throughout the year. It also shows that there had been only a slight improvement in wages for boys since the middle of the century.

It would seem, therefore, that with opportunities for family earnings being gradually eliminated agricultural workers and their families must have remained miserably poor thoughout the nineteenth century and children were encouraged to leave school as soon as the requirements laid down by the Education Acts had been met. This meant that many were still leaving at 11 years old. One of the contributors to the collection of reminiscences published by the Norfolk Federation of Women's Institutes remembers school at Filby in the 1890s:

"Children could leave school when they were eleven years of age, providing they had a job, had made three hundred consecutive attendances for five years and were in Standard V. Many walked four miles to school; they had no milk, no hot dinners, and were very poor. TB was very bad and many children died".[59]

Another man recalled the life of his family at Rollesby in 1900. There were nine children in the family and he was the oldest boy. His father was a bullock worker earning 14s 6d a week, out of which he paid 2s 6d rent.

"My mother had a lot to do at home, and could not earn anything, except a little fruit-picking but in the autumn Mr. Brownsword used to let her go on his meadow, and pick acorns. Us children used to go and help her, and she got ninepence a bushel. We went to school, and we paid for our education in those days, and I took twopence. When I was eleven, there was some talk of getting five shillings a week for my parents from the Parish. They came and asked questions, went into the matter, and the upshot of it was that I had to go out to work. I left school, and started work on a farm for four shillings weekly. So my parents never got the five shillings, they only got four".[60]

A contribution from a man born in Knapton in 1882 reveals a similar pattern:

"I left school when I was twelve, and my first job was at Church Farm . . . I was paid one shilling a week for cleaning shoes, knives and forks and milking the cows and cleaning out stables . . .".[61]

The demand for domestic servants also continued to provide board, lodging and a small wage for the young daughters of poorer families until the social upheaval which resulted from the First World War broke down the class and wealth structures which had enabled even middle-class families to employ staff to run their households. However, certainly up until 1914 and for some years later, it continued to provide a fairly secure and regular occupation for poor girls which reduced the strain on family budgets and living accommodation in the houses of the working-class, as the following recollections show:

> "At the age of fifteen I left home for a big house about thirty miles away, to take my place, as third housemaid in a staff of twelve (almost the lowest form of humanity) for a salary of twelve pounds a year".[62]
>
> Swanton Novers 1917

> "About fifty years ago in Norfolk, all that girls leaving the village school could do was to go into domestic service, more often than not starting as a between maid in a local household, maybe the Hall, the Manor, the Rectory or the doctor's . . . I was to start work on my fourteenth birthday at the doctor's house. For weeks I had been seaming and felling after school hours helping my mother to make my uniform which consisted of two print dresses, six morning aprons, four caps, four afternoon aprons, two blue check aprons, one hessian apron for scrubbing and a black alpaca afternoon dress. My wages were to be one pound a month which had to be taken home to help pay for my outfit".[63]
>
> Blakeney 1920

Although, therefore, the Factory and Education Acts became increasingly effective in protecting children against exploitation throughout the nineteenth century, this threw an almost impossible burden on to the budgets of poor families. The wages of the working-class were still hopelessly inadequate and parents were required to support their children in absolute dependency for an increasing number of years. Protection for children was not accompanied by any scheme which would assist parents to make up the loss of the wages they had earned until the 1940s when the Family Allowances Act, the National Insurance Act, the National Health Service Act and the National Assistance Act were all passed. Thus in the late nineteenth century the family unit was forced to exist without the earnings of children who only fifty years before had been working up to twelve hours a day to supplement the household purse, with no significant improvement in a man's wages to offset this loss.

Increased hardship was almost inevitable, evasions of the law frequent, and it soon became evident that many of the children, who often trudged four or five miles to their nearest school, if not actually starving were certainly under-nourished and inadequately clothed and physically in no condition to derive any lasting benefit from the privilege of free education. One of the first measures taken to counteract this situation was the Education (Provision of Meals) Act in 1906 and this was followed by the duty imposed upon the local education authorities in 1907 to provide for the medical inspection of all children attending public elementary schools. The beginnings of the modern welfare state and a further phase of general social concern for the welfare of children were thus starting to emerge at the outbreak of the First World War.

Conclusion

The children of the poor in nineteenth century Norfolk were born, almost without exception, into a life which was hard, uncertain and marked by unremitting toil. Childhood was a transient moment gone, for most children in the early part of the century, almost before they had emerged from babyhood. They were involved with their parents in a struggle for survival almost as soon as it was physically possible for them to walk to a place of work. In a society which did not see fit to pay its unskilled, or even skilled, workers a wage which allowed them to support their families children became an essential factor in a wage-earning unit which of necessity involved the whole family. They also provided a source of even cheaper labour for the businessmen, landowners and farmers of the period. The pattern of inadequate wages and wretched poverty in the homes of the working-class continued until the early part of the twentieth century, although the gradual emergence of more enlightened and caring attitudes towards children slowly altered the pattern of child labour in the county.

For two-thirds of the century necessity and an absence of any statutory protection for young children created a situation in which boys would start working often as young as five years old, and girls as soon as they could be spared from tasks in the home or could no longer be housed and fed by their parents. During these years occupations for children usually fell into three broad categories – spasmodic or seasonal jobs, full-time work and the employment of whole families. The work they undertook rarely involved training or the acquisition of any real skill, hours were incredibly long and wages miserable.

A boy born in the country would almost certainly begin and end his working life on a farm, starting at five or six years of age doing seasonal jobs like crow-scaring, stone picking, or turnip pulling and cleaning. He would also be involved with the whole family in the work at harvest or perhaps setting and picking potatoes and as he grew older would probably, if he was lucky, get a full-time job doing miscellaneous labouring work. On the coast the pattern would be the same; a variety of intermittent seasonal jobs associated with the fishing industry or on the coastal farms would inevitably be followed by full-time work on the fishing boats or farm labouring by the age of ten or eleven. Here, too, most families would work together at harvest and gleaning time. A wider variety of occupations would be open to a poor city boy but again a picture emerges of "odd" jobs as soon as he was old enough, participation as part of the family wage-earning unit in work connected with the textile industry or perhaps boot and shoe-making, and

ultimately full-time employment in a shop, household or trade in the city. If a little more fortunate he might be apprenticed which would, in theory, at least ensure that a trade or skill was taught and learned. This, however, would have been impossible in the poorest families as it involved the payment of a premium and meant that a boy would earn a very low wage for several years.

For girls the pattern was very similar, although usually they stayed at school for a longer period of time and often they were needed to care for younger children at home so that their mothers might work. In the country, unless they were involved in the dreaded "ganging" system, they occasionally did seasonal jobs on the farms and either helped in the fields with the rest of the family at harvest, or cared for the smaller children at home. On the coast a girl might help her mother mending and drying the nets and in the city, filling bobbins and reels to speed the family work. But, as has been seen, for the girls of city, country and coast full-time domestic service would almost inevitably claim them when the pressure on the family purse and living accommodation became too great.

The change in attitudes which slowly grew throughout this period reached its peak in the last quarter of the century. Compulsory education, accompanied by industrial and agricultural legislation designed to give increasing protection against the exploitation of children, made considerable inroads into the child labour force. It was no longer legal for very little children to be employed and their numbers gradually diminished. Technological improvements in industry and agriculture also affected labour requirements. Thus, the last years of the nineteenth and early years of the twentieth century witnessed the end of the worst aspects of child labour in Norfolk. However, with the lack of any corresponding supportive measures to improve the situation of the working-class family and alleviate the crushing poverty that still existed, schooling for most poor children was something which had to be got through as quickly as it was legally possible. Boys continued to leave school as young as eleven and twelve to take up full-time employment and the girls soon after.

By 1914, therefore, the pattern of child labour in Norfolk had changed quite radically, but the poverty pattern for which most were predestined had scarcely been touched. There would be many more years of long and bitter struggle before the welfare and education of all children was safe-guarded to the point where the pleasure and freedom of childhood could extend beyond the age of eleven years old.

Bibliography

Printed Sources

Ashby, M. K., *The Changing English Village 1066–1914*, The Roundwood Press, 1974.

Baldry, G. (Ed.), Haggard, L. R., *Rabbitskin Cap*, The Boydell Press, 1976 Reprint.

Barrett, W. H., *A Fenman's Story*, Routledge & Kegan Paul, 1965.

Briggs, A., *The Age of Improvement 1783–1867*, Longman, 1974.

Burnett, J. (Ed.), *Useful Toil*, Penguin Books, 1974.

Edwards, G., *From Crow Scaring to Westminster*, Published by The National Union of Agricultural Workers; Printed by Book Plates (PL) Ltd., 1957 Reprint.

Festing, S., *Fishermen*, David & Charles, 1977.

Green, B. & Young, R. M. R., *Norwich–The Growth of a City*, Norfolk Museums Service, 1975 Reprint.

Haggard, L. R. (Ed.), *I Walked by Night*, The Boydell Press, 1976 Reprint.

Horn, P., *The Victorian Country Child*, The Roundwood Press, 1974.

Musgrave, P. W., *Society and Education in England since 1800*, Methuen, 1968.

Norfolk Federation of Women's Institutes, *Within Living Memory*, The Boydell Press, 1973.

Page, R. (Ed.), *Census of Norwich 1851 – Part One – St. Martin-at-Palace, St. Martin-at-Oak*, Norfolk and Norwich Genealogical Society, 1975.

Pinchbeck, I, & Hewitt, M., *Children in English Society Vol. II*, Routledge & Kegan Paul, 1973.

Randell, A. (Ed.), Porter, E., *Sixty Years a Fenman*, Routledge & Kegan Paul, 1965.

Samuel, R. (Ed.), *Village Life and Labour*, Routledge & Kegan Paul, 1975.

Springall, L. M., *Labouring Life in Norfolk Villages 1834–1914*, George Allen & Unwin Ltd., 1936.

Thomson, D., *England in the Nineteenth Century*, Penguin Books, 1977 Reprint.

Manuscript Sources

Committee Books of the Boy's Home attached to the Norwich Workhouse, 1855–1862, Norfolk & Norwich Record Office, N/TC 3/87.

Committee Books of the Girls' Home attached to the Norwich Workhouse, 1857–1863, Norfolk & Norwich Record Office, N/TC 3/88.

Diary or Log Book of Felthorpe School, Norfolk, 1867–1896, Norfolk & Norwich Record Office, C/ED 2/2.

Diary or Log Book of Ranworth-with-Panxworth School, Norfolk, 1874–1883, Norfolk & Norwich Record Office, C/ED 2/109.

Diary or Log Book of Snetterton National School, Norfolk, 1873–1896, Norfolk & Norwich Record Office, C/ED 2/64.

Diary or Log Book of Westacre School, Norfolk, 1876–1897, Norfolk & Norwich Record Office, C/ED 2/16.

Recollections of Hunstanton Hall 1846–1853 by Jamesina Waller (née L'Estrange), Norfolk and Norwich Record Office, MS.21219 T 140 C.

Springall, L. M., *The Norfolk Agricultural Labourer 1834–1884*, London University Ph.D. thesis 1935, Colman & Rye Library, Norwich.

Account Book of Testerton Hall Farm, Norfolk, 1899–1900, in private possession.

References

Note: titles listed in Bibliography are cited by author

[1] Townsend, J. '*A Dissertation on the Poor Laws (1786)*' quoted in Briggs p.16.
[2] Pinchbeck and Hewitt p.358.
[3] Springall p.64
[4] *Log Book of Ranworth-with-Panxworth School 1874–1883*, Norfolk & Norwich Record Office, C/ED 2/109.
[5] *Log Book of Felthorpe School 1876–1896*, Norfolk & Norwich Record Office, C/ED 2/2.
[6] Baldry pp. 34 and 42.
[7] Edwards p.25.
[8] Haggard p.25.
[9] Baldry pp. 91 and 93.
[10] Edwards p.23.
[11] Ibid. pp. 25 and 26.
[12] Ibid. p.24.
[13] Randell pp. 22 and 23.
[14] Barrett pp. 3 and 4.
[15] *Log Book of Westacre School 1876–1897*, Norfolk & Norwich Record Office, C/ED 2/16.
[16-19] *Log Book of Snetterton National School 1873–1896*, Norfolk & Norwich Record Office, C/ED 2/64.
[20] Kitteringham, J. '*Country Work Girls in Nineteenth Century England*' in Samuel p.97.
[21] Reader, W. J. in Horn p. 114.
[22] Log Book op. cit.
[23] Springall p.43.
[24] Pinchbeck and Hewitt pp. 392 and 393.
[25] Horn pp. 122 and 123.
[26] Festing p.43.
[27] Ibid. p.39.
[28] Ibid. p.121.
[29] Ibid. p.138.
[30] Ibid. p.133.
[31-35] Page
[36] 1851 Census quoted in Horn p.121.
[37] Page
[38] Waller, J. (née L'Estrange) '*Recollections of Hunstanton Hall 1846–1853*, Norfolk & Norwich Record Office, MS.21219 T 140 C.
[39] Pinchbeck and Hewitt p.501.

[40-51] *Committee Books of the Boys' Home attached to the Norwich Workhouse 1855–1862*, Norfolk & Norwich Record Office N/TC 3/87

[52-56] *Committee Books of the Girls' Home attached to the Norwich Workhouse 1857–1863*, Norfolk & Norwich Record Office, N/TC 3/88.

[57] Norfolk Federation of Women's Institutes p.104.

[58] *Account Book. Testerton Hall Farm, 1899–1900*, in private possession.

[59] Norfolk Federation of Women's Institutes p.104.

[60] Ibid. p.71.

[61] Ibid. p.74.

[62] Ibid. p.92.

[63] Ibid. pp. 92 and 93.